# Animal Classification

## Do Cats Have Family Trees?

Eve Hartman and Wendy Meshbesher

raintree

a Capstone company — publishers for children

Raintree is an imprint of Capstone Global Library Limited, a company incorporated in England and Wales having its registered office at 7 Pilgrim Street, London, EC4V 6LB – Registered company number: 6695582

www.raintreepublishers.co.uk
myorders@raintreepublishers.co.uk

Edited by Adam Miller, Sian Smith and Penny West
Designed by Philippa Jenkins
Picture research by Tracy Cummins
Originated by Capstone Global Library Ltd
Produced by Victoria Fitzgerald
Printed and bound in China by CTPS

ISBN 978 1 406 27432 5 (hardback)
17 16 15 14 13
10 9 8 7 6 5 4 3 2 1

ISBN 978 1 406 27439 4 (paperback)
18 17 16 15 14
10 9 8 7 6 5 4 3 2 1

Hartman, Eve and Meshbesher, Wendy
Animal Classification: Do Cats Have Family Trees? (Show Me Science)
A full catalogue record for this book is available from the British Library.

## Acknowledgements
We would like to thank the following for permission to reproduce photographs:
Getty Images pp. 8 (Visuals Unlimited, Inc./Science Stills/ARS), 9 (Monty Rakusen), 10 (Visuals Unlimited, Inc./ Wim van Egmond), 18 (mcb bank bhalwal), 21 (Charlie Tyack Photography), 24 left (MariaR); Istockphoto pp.5 bottom (Fenykepez), 7 (Fenykepez), 15 bottom (Jeremy Lang), 15 middle (John Kaprielian / Science Source); Shutterstock pp. 5, 11 bottom (© Andrew Orlemann), 11 top (© Chantal de Bruijne), 12 (© Semjonow Juri), 14 (© Cathy Keifer), 15 top (© Eduardo Rivero), 19 bottom (© David Thyberg), 19 top (© Arnold John Labrentz), 20 (© Critterbiz), 22 (© Angel's Gate Photography), 24 right (© Vasiliy Koval), 25 (© BasPhoto), 28 (© Eric Isselee), 28 left (© Matt Gore); Superstock 13 (Fleetman/VWPics), 16 (F1 ONLINE), 17 bottom (NHPA), 17 top (Animals Animals).

Cover photograph reproduced with permission of Getty Images (Martin Ruegner).

We would like to thank Michael Bright for his invaluable help in the preparation of this book.
Every effort has been made to contact copyright holders of material reproduced in this book. Any omissions will be rectified in subsequent printings if notice is given to the publishers.

## Disclaimer
All the Internet addresses (URLs) given in this book were valid at the time of going to press. However, due to the dynamic nature of the Internet, some addresses may have changed, or sites may have changed or ceased to exist since publication. While the author and publishers regret any inconvenience this may cause readers, no responsibility for any such changes can be accepted by either the author or the publishers.

# Contents

Some words are shown in bold, **like this**. You can find out what they mean by looking in the glossary.

Fluffy is a kitten. She is only a few weeks old. Fluffy knows the cat that is her mother. She also has a father and brother and sister kittens.

Fluffy has other family, too. Her mother and father each had two parents. These parents also had two parents, and so did their parents. A diagram that shows parents and children is called a **family tree**. Like a real tree, a family tree has many branches that are all connected.

Fluffy's family tree includes the 19 cats shown here. But the whole tree is much larger. The whole tree includes more parent cats, and their parents, and more parents beyond that.

## More family for Fluffy

We could add even more cats to Fluffy's family tree. Look at page 5 and find Fluffy's parents, who are Samuel and Honey. We could add their sisters and brothers to the tree. These cats are Fluffy's aunts and uncles. The kittens of the aunts and uncles are Fluffy's cousins.

Next, we could add all of the brothers and sisters of Fluffy's grandparents and great-grandparents. Then we could add their kittens, and then the grandkittens.

As you can see, Fluffy's real family tree is very, very big!

Oscar Fiona Max Pixie Harry Trixie Snowy Pook

Reuben Belle Peter Bridgie

Samuel Honey

Fluffy

Fluffy's family tree shows how she is related to family members. Trace the line that connects Fluffy to Pixie. How are they related?

Fergus

Soupy Slinky Simon

Look again at Fluffy's **family tree** on page 5. Then compare it to the diagram on page 7. This diagram is sometimes called the tree of life.

Fluffy's family tree shows cats only, but the tree of life shows many kinds of living things. Its branches represent all life on Earth!

To **classify** is to put things into groups. Scientists use family trees and family relationships to classify life. They do so because all living things are related. The first **organism**, or individual living thing, appeared billions of years ago. On the tree of life, this ancient organism would be placed at the bottom of the tree.

## Species

A **species** is a kind of living thing. All house cats are members of the same species. There are many species of fish and birds, and many more species of insects. Scientists think that Earth is home to about nine million species.

To classify species, scientists organize them into groups. The box (right) shows the set of groups that classify Fluffy the cat. You will learn about each of these groups in this book.

| | |
|---|---|
| **SPECIES:** | *Felis catus* (house cat) |
| **GENUS:** | *Felis* (small cat) |
| **FAMILY:** | Feline (cat) |
| **ORDER:** | Carnivore |
| **CLASS:** | Mammal |
| **PHYLUM:** | Chordate (SUBPHYLUM: Vertebrate) |
| **KINGDOM:** | Animal |
| **DOMAIN:** | Eukaryote |

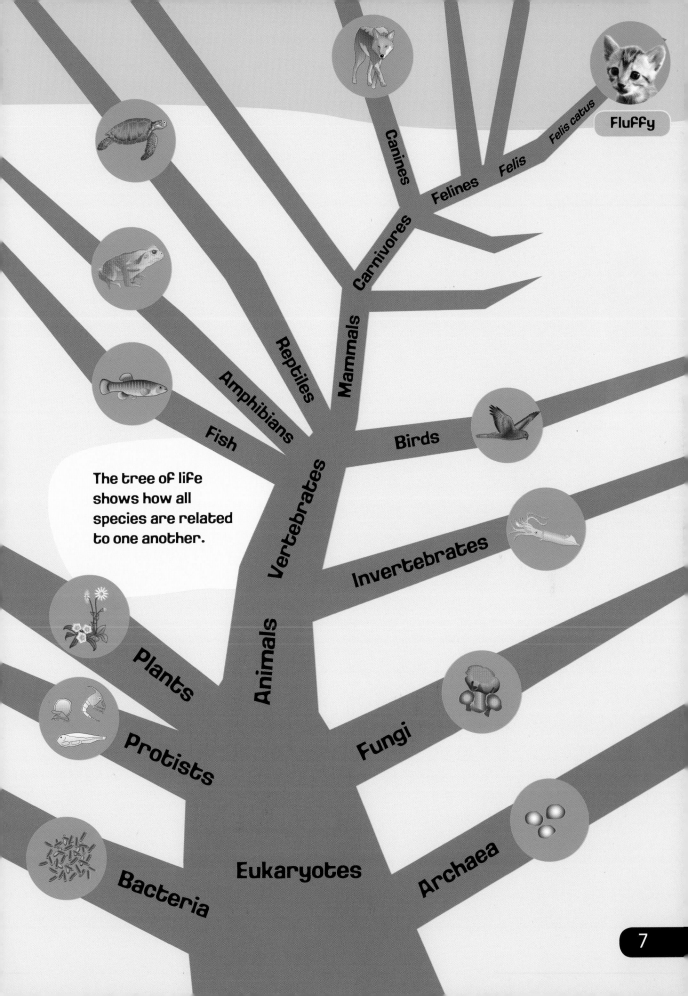

The tree of life shows how all species are related to one another.

Fluffy

Felis catus

Felis

Felines

Canines

Carnivores

Mammals

Reptiles

Amphibians

Birds

Fish

Vertebrates

Invertebrates

Plants

Animals

Protists

Fungi

Bacteria

Eukaryotes

Archaea

# Domains

A **domain** is the largest group of living things. The three domains are archaea, bacteria, and eukaryotes. Each **species** is a member of one of these three domains.

Both archaea and bacteria are very simple forms of life. The **organisms** of these groups are made of one **cell** only. A cell is a tiny unit of life. All organisms are made of cells.

Some eukaryotes are made of one cell only. But the group also includes all living things that are made of more than one cell. Fluffy and other cats are eukaryotes. So are humans, other animals, and plants.

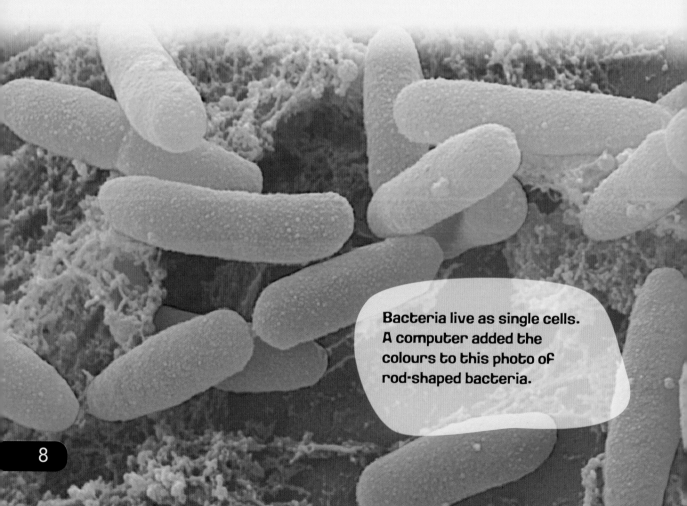

Bacteria live as single cells. A computer added the colours to this photo of rod-shaped bacteria.

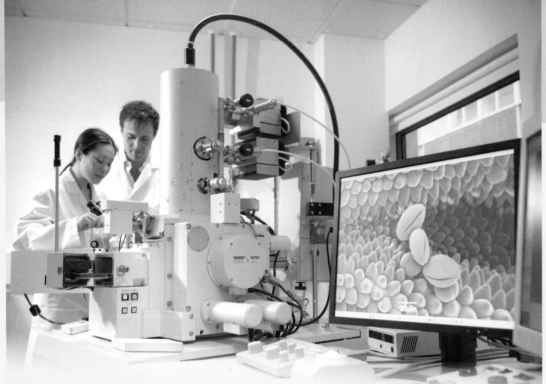

## Microscopes

Cells are too small to see without a microscope. A microscope is a tool that makes images appear larger. Scientists discovered cells soon after the first microscopes were invented in the 1600s. Today, we use very powerful microscopes to study cells and **classify** bacteria.

## JOSEPH LISTER

Before the 1800s, a visit to the doctor often caused more harm than good. The doctor might stitch together a wound. But after a week or so, the wound sometimes turned an ugly colour. Patients then got a high fever, and sometimes they died. British surgeon Joseph Lister thought that bacteria or other germs were causing these problems. He tried to keep wounds and instruments very clean. He thought that cleanliness would stop bacteria from taking hold. Lister was right! Today, surgeons always operate under sterile (germ-free) conditions.

A **kingdom** is the next largest group. The eukaryotes are grouped into four kingdoms. They are the protists, fungi, plants, and animals.

## Protists

Like bacteria, most protists are made of one **cell** only. But protist cells are larger and more complex. Many protists live in pond water. Others live in the soil. Some protists eat food as they move from place to place. They act like tiny animals. Other protists make their own food. They act like tiny plants.

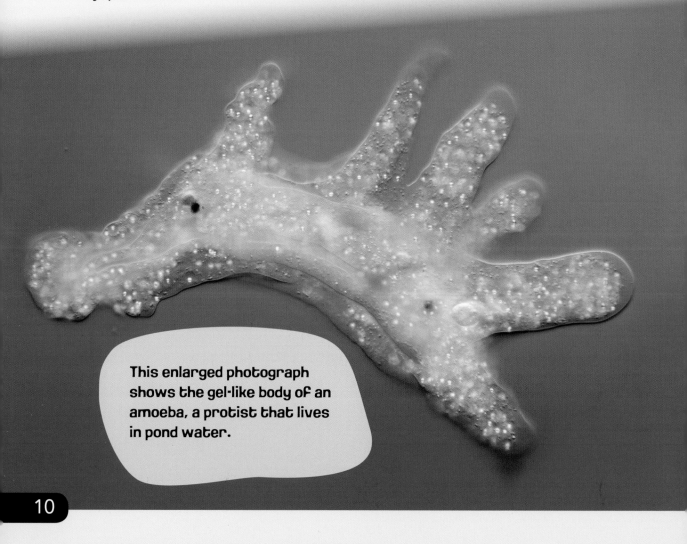

This enlarged photograph shows the gel-like body of an amoeba, a protist that lives in pond water.

A few mushrooms are good to eat. But never pick and eat wild mushrooms. Some are poisonous!

## Fungi

Mushrooms are members of the fungi kingdom. So are yeasts, which are used to bake bread. Fungi get food by breaking down dead plants or animals. Many live in forest soils, getting food from dead wood and fallen leaves.

## Plants

Some plants, like moss, will fit in the palm of your hand. But the largest plants tower over houses. Trees are among the tallest, largest, and heaviest of Earth's **organisms**.

Plants make their own food. They have green parts, such as leaves and needles. The green parts take in air, water, and sunlight. They use the energy of sunlight to turn air and water into food.

## What's oldest?

What is Earth's oldest living organism? Scientists think the bristlecone pine shown here is over 4,000 years old. But it is less than half the age of some Norway spruce trees that live in Sweden.

# Meet the animals

Fluffy and other cats are members of the animal **kingdom**. Unlike plants and fungi, animals eat their food. Without plants to make food, all animals would quickly die.

Scientists divide animals into two main groups. **Vertebrates** are animals with **backbones**. Cats are vertebrates, as are humans and most other large animals. **Invertebrates** do not have backbones.

## Invertebrates

Invertebrates include most of the small animals that crawl, wriggle, or fly. The invertebrates that live on land include worms, snails, and insects. In the ocean are sponges, jellies, and clams. Squids and octopuses are the largest invertebrates.

Bees are invertebrates. Their visits to flowers help plants make seeds.

# The amazing octopus

When an octopus is hunting, it often changes its shape or colour to blend into the background. We do not know how they make these decisions.

An octopus also has a kind of second brain in each of its arms. One scientist saw an octopus lose an arm. The cut-off arm caught a fish. The arm tried to bring the fish to where the mouth would have been.

If you could count all the animals alive today, most would be insects. Some insects, like fleas, might annoy our friend Fluffy. But other insects fill useful roles. Bees help flowers form seeds. Silk moths make silk, a kind of fabric. Insects also are food for larger animals.

A scientist named Peter Godfrey-Smith once said,

*"Meeting an octopus is like meeting an intelligent alien."*

Scientists divide the **vertebrates** into smaller groups called **classes**. Fluffy's class, **mammals**, is covered on pages 16 and 17. Other classes are fish, **amphibians**, **reptiles**, and birds.

## Fish

Fish get the **oxygen** they need to live through parts called **gills**. Gills take in oxygen that mixes from the air into the water. Most fish also have fins, and the bodies of many are covered in scales. Fins and scales help them swim.

## Amphibians

Frogs and toads are amphibians. They begin their lives in water. Then their bodies change and they grow **lungs** to breathe oxygen from the air. They also grow legs so they can move from water to land.

## Reptiles

Snakes, lizards, and turtles are reptiles. So are alligators and crocodiles. Most reptiles live on land from birth. They lay hard, leathery eggs that do not dry out in the air. Their bodies are covered in hard scales or plates.

This chameleon, has brightly coloured scales.

All birds have beaks. The long beak of the toucan is ideal for eating fruit.

# Birds

Every bird has two wings, two feet, a beak, and a body covered in feathers. Most birds are light enough to fly. Other birds swim or run.

# Is Fluffy like a fish?

Fluffy looks and acts differently from a fish. But they have a few things in common. Both have a head and a tail joined to a long **backbone**. Now compare the cat's ribs with the thin bones of the fish. Both sets of bones are attached to the spine.

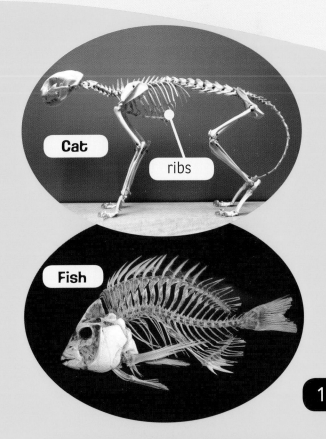

Cat

ribs

Fish

# Mammals

Now let's look at Fluffy's **class**, the **mammals**. Mammals have hair. They also make milk to feed their young. Most mammals are born instead of hatching from eggs.

Some mammals live in cold, snowy places. Their hair, fur, and fat help keep their bodies warm. Mammals also live in warmer places, including forests, deserts, and grasslands.

Whales and dolphins are mammals that live in the ocean. They must come to the surface to breathe. All mammals breathe air through their **lungs**.

Female mammals make milk for their young.

The first mammals looked a bit like this tree shrew.

## The first mammals

Scientists think the first mammals appeared about 200 million years ago. They were small and hairy, and they ate insects.

For millions of years, mammals stayed small in size and few in number. Dinosaurs, which were **reptiles**, were Earth's largest animals, and they ate most of the food. Then all the dinosaurs died suddenly. Scientists think the cause was a large rock from space that struck Earth. Only then did mammals begin to grow in variety, size, and number.

## The oddest mammal?

The oddest mammal might be the platypus. Like all mammals, the platypus has hair and makes milk for its young. But the young hatch from eggs. The platypus also has a bird's beak and webbed feet. If you meet a male platypus, watch out for its back leg. It has a spike that delivers painful **venom**.

# Orders of mammals

The members of a **class** are divided into more groups, called **orders**. Look at the table, where some orders are listed. Can you guess Fluffy's order?

| Order | Examples | Order | Examples |
|---|---|---|---|
| Artiodactyls | giraffes, deer, cattle, pigs | Monotremes | echidnas, platypuses |
| Carnivores | wolves, dogs, bears, raccoons | Perissodactyls | horses, rhinoceroses |
| Cetaceans | whales, dolphins | Primates | lemurs, monkeys, humans |
| Chiropterans | bats | Proboscids | elephants |
| Dermopterans | flying lemurs | Rodents | mice, rats, squirrels, gophers |
| Hyracoids | hyraxes | | |
| Lagomorphs | rabbits, hares | Sirenians | manatees |

## Rodents

Mice and rats are rodents. So are larger animals like gophers, porcupines, and beavers. All rodents have sharp front teeth that are always growing longer. To wear these teeth down, rodents eat seeds.

## Bats

Bats are the only **mammals** that can fly (though some can glide). Their wings are made of thin skin that tears easily, but mends quickly. Many kinds of bats catch and eat insects. Others eat fruit.

# Animals of Madagascar

Madagascar is an island off the Southeast coast of Africa. It is home to many animals that live nowhere else in the world. Scientists continue to discover new **species** there. One is the pocket lemur, a primate that fits in the palm of your hand.

## Primates

Monkeys, apes, and lemurs are **classified** as primates. Humans are also in this order. Primates have hands that can grasp objects. They have two eyes that face forward. Many primates walk well on two legs.

## Hoofed mammals

Hooves are like strong, sturdy shoes – useful for walking on hard ground. Mammals with hooves are grouped in two orders. Giraffes, deer, cattle, sheep, and pigs are some of the animals in one order. Horses, zebras, and rhinoceroses are in the other order. All hoofed mammals walk on four legs.

Long legs and hooves help this moose walk on hard, rocky ground.

# Meet the meat-eaters!

The word "carnivore" means "meat-eater". Did you guess that Fluffy is a carnivore? All cats are members of the carnivore **order**. So are wolves and dogs.

Being a carnivore helps to explain Fluffy's behaviour. Fluffy likes to chase small things that move, such as a rolling ball of wool. This is good practice for catching a mouse or a baby bird! In the wild, cats live by catching and eating small animals. Pet cats sometimes do this, too.

Wolves often live in groups called packs.

## Food for Fluffy

Pet food companies make and sell many kinds of cat food. Some cat food contains only meat. Others have meat mixed with grains. If you own a pet, talk to a pet shop owner about the different kinds of food for sale. Or ask a vet (animal doctor) about pet food. The right food can help your pet lead a happy, healthy life.

## What big teeth you have!

How can you tell a carnivore from other **mammals**? One way is to look inside its mouth. Carnivores have several sharp, pointed teeth, like those shown in the photograph. These teeth are useful for biting **prey** (hunted animals) and tearing meat. Plant-eating animals have rows of flat teeth, which they use for grinding.

# The cat family

An **order** is divided into smaller groups, called **families**. All cats are members of the same family, called the **felines**. Dogs and wolves are grouped in a different family, the **canines**.

Lions are the largest felines. Compare the appearances of the female lion (left) and the male.

# The lion's mane

A mane is a patch of long hair on the neck. The male lion is the only adult cat that has a mane. A baby cheetah also has a mane.

The felines include many cats that are much larger than Fluffy. Lions, tigers, and cheetahs are all felines. So are jaguars, pumas, and leopards. In nature, all felines hunt other animals for food. They have sharp claws and keen eyesight. They are fast runners, too.

Some felines, like lions, often live together in groups. They work together to hunt large **prey**. Other felines, like tigers, usually live by themselves. A mother tiger will show her cubs how to hunt. Then she will leave them and live alone again.

## The litter box

Would you let a chicken run around your house? If so, you might find its droppings almost everywhere. But you can easily train a cat to use a litter box. Why? Scientists think that house cats came from wildcats of the Middle East. The land there is very sandy. Wildcats bury their droppings in the sand to hide the smell. Otherwise, enemies might find them.

Pets like Fluffy might never meet an animal that wants to eat them. Nevertheless, they practice the same behaviours that wildcats once used to stay safe.

# Genus and species

As you have discovered, Fluffy is an animal, a **vertebrate**, and a **mammal**. She also is a carnivore and a **feline**. We are now ready to place Fluffy into two smaller groups. These groups are called **genus** and **species**.

Though some cats look different, they are still the same species.

Birman

Siamese

# CATS IN EGYPT

In ancient Egypt, cats were prized for killing snakes and other pests. The goddess Bastet was shown as a woman with the head of a cat. She was thought to protect homes and new mothers.

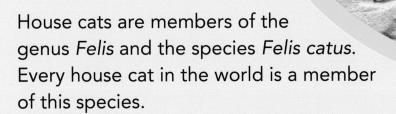

House cats are members of the genus *Felis* and the species *Felis catus*. Every house cat in the world is a member of this species.

Animals in the same species are able to **mate** with one another. Their young are able to mate and have young of their own.

## Breeds

Do animals of the same species all look alike? Often they do not. Compare the two examples of *Felis catus* shown opposite. The Birman cat has a round face and body, and its hair is long and white. The Siamese, however, has a long, thin face and short hair.

These two cats are members of different **breeds**. A breed is a small group within a species. People often develop breeds by choosing which adults to mate. Breeds of cats, dogs, horses, and cattle have all developed this way.

# Fluffy and her family

**Classifying** living things helps us to understand how they live and grow. We classify Fluffy as a member of *Felis catus*. This helps us to predict which foods Fluffy should eat, and which she should avoid. We also can predict how she will change as she gets older, and how long she will live. If Fluffy becomes ill, vets can use their knowledge of *Felis catus* to treat her.

When scientists discover an **organism** they do not recognize, their first task is to classify it. Is it a plant or an animal? If it is an animal, does it have a **backbone**? Does it have **gills** or **lungs**? Is its body covered in scales, feathers, or hair? The answers help to name the **species** and place it on the tree of life.

## Always changing

Fluffy's life is always changing. Her family is always changing, too. As Fluffy grows older, she may have kittens of her own. The kittens will look and act a lot like Fluffy and her parents, but not exactly like them. They might be larger or smaller, thinner or fatter, or have different markings on their fur. Like Fluffy's family, the tree of life also changes over time. The changes take place slowly, often over many thousands or millions of years. But eventually, older species give rise to new ones.

| | | |
|---|---|---|
| **DOMAIN** | **Eukaryote** | **Has many cells that work together** |
| **KINGDOM** | **Animal** | **Eats food; moves from place to place** |
| **PHYLUM** | **Chordate** | **SUBPHYLUM: Vertebrate - has a backbone** |
| **CLASS** | **Mammal** | **Has hair or fur; makes milk for its young** |
| **ORDER** | **Carnivore** | **Eats meat** |
| **FAMILY** | **Feline (cat)** | **Has claws and keen senses; fast runner** |
| **GENUS** | *Felis* **(small cat)** | **Small in size** |
| **SPECIES** | *Felis catus* **(house cat)** | **Can be easy to tame** |

We can show the family members of Fluffy the cat – or any other animal – in a diagram called a **family tree**. Like a real tree, a family tree has many branches that are all connected. Scientists use diagrams like family trees to show how all living things are related.

Every living thing is **classified** into several groups. The largest group is called a **domain**. All plants, fungi, and animals are classified together in the same domain. The smaller groups are **kingdom**, **phylum**, **class**, **order**, **family**, **genus**, and **species**. Members of the same species can **mate** with one another to make more of their own kind.

# Quiz

## 1

All plants and animals are members of the same:
A. kingdom
B. domain
C. class
D. species

(See page 8)

## 2

An octopus is an invertebrate because it:
A. lives in the ocean
B. hunts for food
C. has no backbone
D. has soft skin

(See page 12)

## 3

The platypus is classified as a:
A. bird
B. fish
C. reptile
D. mammal

(See page 17)

## 4

Members of the same order as Fluffy the cat are:
A. wolves
B. mice
C. rabbits
D. cows

(See page 20)

## 5

*Felis catus* is the name of Fluffy's:
A. breed
B. species
C. phylum
D. order

(See page 25)

(Answers: 1B; 2C; 3D; 4A; 5B)

**amphibian** vertebrate that begins life in water and then may live on land

**backbone** bony part of the body that runs down from the head

**breed** small group within a species of animal

**canine** group within a family that includes dogs

**cell** tiny unit that all living things are made out of

**class** group within a phylum

**classify** put things into groups

**domain** one of three large groups of living things

**family** group within an order

**family tree** diagram that shows how parents and children are related

**feline** group within a family that includes cats

**genus** group within a family

**gills** body parts that fish use to breathe

**invertebrate** animal without a backbone

**kingdom** one of six groups used to classify living things

**lung** organ in the body where oxygen moves into the blood, and carbon dioxide moves out of the blood

**mammal** member of the group of animals with hair on their bodies, whose young feed on their mother's milk

**mate** when animals come together in order to have young

**order** group within a class

**organism** individual living thing

**oxygen** gas that is part of the air; needed by all plants and animals

**phylum** group smaller than a kingdom, but bigger than a class

**prey** animal that is hunted, caught, and eaten by another animal

**reptile** vertebrate that lays leathery eggs and has scaly skin

**species** kind of living thing; members of a species can breed to make more members

**venom** poison produced by some animals

**vertebrate** animal with a backbone

# Find out more

## Books

*Cat* (DK Eyewitness), Juliet Clutton-Brock (DK Children, 2004)

*Classifying Reptiles* (Classifying Living Things), Richard and Louise Spilsbury (Heinemann Library, 2009)

*Dogs* (Animal Family Albums), Paul Mason (Raintree, 2013)

*Tree of Life: The Incredible Biodiversity of Life on Earth*, Rochelle Strauss (A & C Black , 2008)

*A Whale is Not a Fish and Other Animal Mix-Ups*, Melvin Berger (Scholastic, 1996)

## Websites

**www.biology4kids.com/files/micro_bacteria.html**
Learn about the lives of bacteria, which are organisms too small to see without a microscope. Find out how bacteria affect your life, in both helpful and harmful ways

**www.nationalgeographic.com/features/97/cats**
This National Geographic website helps you explore members of the cat family, including pet cats and cats that live in the wild.

**www.nationalzoo.si.edu**
Discover facts about all sorts of animals, from the National Zoo in Washington DC, USA.

**www.paws.org/kids-about-cats.html**
Here you can learn some surprising and interesting facts about your favourite house pet. Or if you prefer dogs, click on the link to learn about them.